WASHINGTON
SHORES

WASHINGTON SHORES

PHOTOGRAPHY BY DAVID MUENCH • TEXT BY SPENCER GILL

Right: Shells and old processing building on pilings in Oysterville tideflats bear witness to the oyster industry for which Willapa Bay has been famous since the 1850s. Small native oysters have been supplanted by the larger Pacific species.

International Standard Book Number: 0-912856-68-8

Library of Congress Number: 80-85369

Copyright© by Graphic Arts Center Publishing Company

Post Office Box 10306, Portland, Oregon 97210 (503) 224-7777

Publisher • Charles H. Belding

Designer • Robert Reynolds

Typesetting • Paul O. Giesey/Adcrafters

Printer • Graphic Arts Center

Binding • Lincoln & Allen

Printed in the United States of America

Ilwaco, on Baker Bay just inside the mouth of the Columbia River, is protected by headlands to the west, providing a quiet harbor for boats and fishermen. *Left:* Coastal backwaters in shaded woods, such as this section in Fort Canby State Park, with skunk cabbage, ferns and pond grasses provide habitat and food for a myriad of land and water creatures. *Pages 8 and 9:* Warning of rocks and shoals and the Columbia bar, Cape Disappointment lighthouse stands on the point where Lewis and Clark first viewed the Pacific in 1805. The first lighthouse signaling the entrance to the Columbia was erected on the cape in 1856.

North Head looms above storm-darkened seas near Dead Man's Hollow, named for the crew of the *Vandalia,* lost when the ship foundered off the mouth of the Columbia in 1853. *Right:* Golden leaves of vine maple signal the arrival of autumn and seasonal rains. The sprawling branches of this small tree reach out in all directions, joining with elderberry and salmonberry in the tangled underbrush of Northwest evergreen forests. *Pages 12 and 13:* Big-leaf maples, which grow along river banks and below towering spruce and hemlock, are favored dwelling places for mosses, lichens and ferns.

A pinnacle, undercut by water and weather, stands like a forested schooner
in the marshlands off the east shore of Willapa Bay near the mouth of the Nemah
River. *Left:* In time, backwaters and former riverbeds can become new forest
lands as decaying vegetation and silt accumulate, providing a base for
successive growths of grasses and sedges, willows and alders, then larger trees.

Club mosses and lichens drape the trees and ferns carpet the ground in the forest just north of Willapa National Wildlife Refuge. *Right:* Waves move onshore near the coastal boundary of the Quinault Indian Reservation and beat against the sea stack which was once part of the headland.

Storm waves break against the promontory named Point Grenville by Captain Vancouver in 1792. In 1775, the Spanish explorers Heceta and Bodega y Quadra called it Point of the Martyrs after several crew members seeking water on shore were ambushed by Indians. *Left:* Gulls and sandpipers in the Taholah area are just two of some 75 species of seabirds and shorebirds which are year-round residents or migratory visitors along the coastal shores. *Pages 20 and 21:* Second Beach, on the coastal section of Olympic National Park, offers great sea stacks and rich tide pools; safest access is by a long forest trail which leads off from the road to La Push.

Elephant Rock and Tunnel Island where the Raft River enters the Pacific, are
intriguing and awesome memorials to the erosive power of the seas. *Left:* At
Beach #4, near Kalaloch, starfish and anemones share a rock with its
permanent residents, the barnacles. The beach is also shared by clam diggers,
surf fishermen and smelt netters. *Pages 24-25:* During winter storms, these
now-gentle waves at Third Beach can become marauding giants picking up drift
logs and hurling them against the sandy shore and rocky headlands with
thunderous force.

Storms at sea churn the waves and bring layers of sea foam to the beaches. *Right:* Rain, sun, waves and wind have bleached and patterned this cedar drift log. *Pages 28 and 29:* Shi Shi Beach, remote and difficult of access, offers tide pools to study, wave-sculpted tunnels and caves to explore and miles of sandy shore to walk between Point of Arches and Portage Head.

Sea stacks near Cape Flattery will ultimately succumb to the ceaseless grinding of the sand-laden waves, the same unrelenting force which shaped them. *Left:* Giant's Graveyard is the name given to the group of high rocks in the ocean near Teahwhit Head. These sea stacks were once part of the coast, cut away by the erosive action of the Pacific.

Stylized painting of a whale decorates a boat at La Push, a salmon fishing harbor and village on the Quillayute Indian Reservation. The name is from the Chinook jargon version of the French trappers "la bouche" for "the mouth" of the Quillayute River which enters the Pacific here. *Right:* Rialto Beach, on the coastal stretch of Olympic National Park, is partly covered by smooth pebbles and stones which show the polishing action of waves and sand.

Storm-driven waves carry huge logs and driftwood onto the coastal shores, as here on Rialto Beach. Mist and fog are frequent companions at the shore. *Left:* Starfish, like this one on the wet sand at Second Beach, are more commonly found clinging to rocks in tidepools and at the base of sea stacks; this may have been pulled from its usual home and discarded. *Pages 36 and 37:* Neah Bay is a fishing port and headquarters of the Makah Indian Reservation. For centuries the Makahs excelled as canoe-makers and hunters of seal and whale, venturing from here far into the ocean in their cedar dugouts.

Makah symbols of thunderbird, whale and bear are displayed in this contemporary rendering on a wood wall at Neah Bay. *Right:* Brown sea sac algae and rockweed are exposed at low tide on Indian Island near Cape Alava. It is also known as Cannonball Island because of the "cannonballs" or large, spherical rocks, which some geologists indicate are sandstone concretions washed out of the cliffs and made round by ancient waves. *Pages 40 and 41:* Drift logs form a similar pattern and frame the sea-sculptured rocks near Cape Johnson.

Only means of land access to many Northwest coast beaches, such as this one near Sand Point, are forest trails leading sometimes for miles through tall, moss-covered trees, ferns, salal and salmonberry. *Left:* Totem pole at the Neah Bay cemetery on the edge of the Makah Reservation becomes an intriguing display of overlapping symbols through the photographer's creative use of double-exposure. *Pages 44 and 45:* Silhouettes of sea stacks form a monumental pattern near Cape Flattery, the northwest tip of the Olympic Peninsula and the southern entrance to the Strait of Juan de Fuca.

Wave-scalloped formations, pools, rocks and sea stacks are typical of the northern shores of Olympic National Park. *Right:* View through the narrow opening in the high edge of the shore near Cape Flattery presents a dramatic picture of how the tidal waters cut through the rocks to create sea stacks.

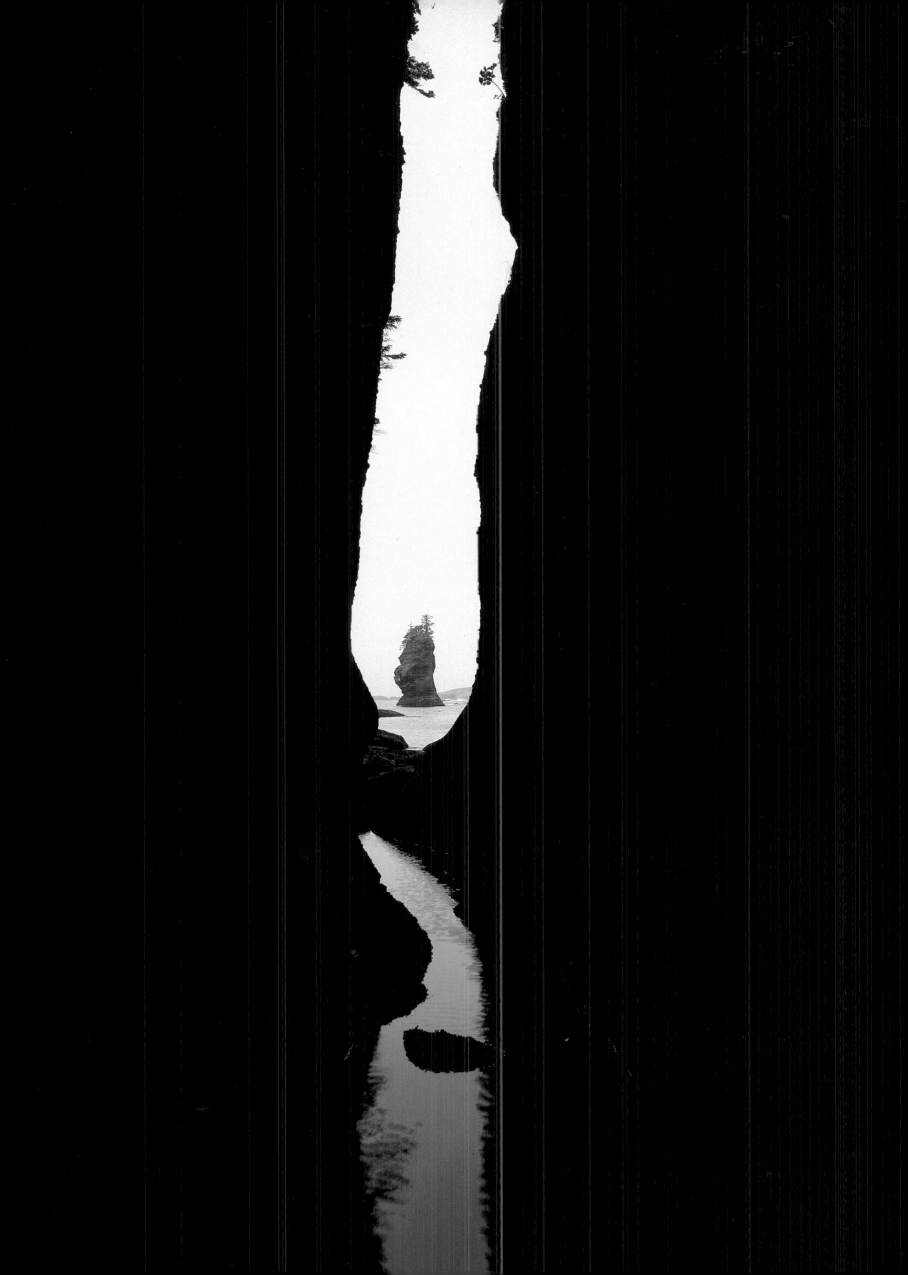

Lake Crescent lies in a tranquil alpine setting of forested slopes in Olympic National Park. The 600-foot-deep lake offers fishing for trout, including, it is said, a unique species of landlocked salmon. *Left:* Soleduck River is one of the longest and loveliest of streams flowing from headwaters in Olympic National Forest; it joins with the Bogachiel to form the Quillayute River which then travels six miles to the Pacific.

Tidal waters swirl at the base of Cape Flattery, named by Captain James Cook in 1778, when he noted in the shore: "a small opening which flattered us with the hopes of finding a harbour there." *Right:* Tatoosh Island, at the Washington shore entrance to Strait of Juan de Fuca, has held a lighthouse since 1857. The island was named by John Meares in 1788. *Pages 52 and 53:* Mount Olympus at 7,965 feet is highest peak in the rugged Olympic Range and carries the burden of seven ancient glaciers which are continually provided new ice crystals by the moisture-laden winds from the Pacific.

Warm, moist winds from the ocean bring mi d temperatures and as much as 12 feet of rain each year to the westerly-facing valleys of the Olympics, such as the Hoh, Queets, Bogachiel and Quinault, creating conditions for growth as lush as in tropical rain forests. *Left:* Beneath the towering evergreens in the Hoh Rain Forest, tall big-leaf maples are festooned with club moss, adorned with lichens and ferns. Olympic National Park naturalists refer to this part of the forest as the Hall of Mosses. *Pages 56 and 57:* Vegetation and birds of the sea coast are reminders that tidal waters wash the shores of the Strait of Juan de Fuca.

Skunk cabbage, fern, alder, maple and shade-tolerant plants which like moisture grow in abundance on forest floors and wet lands of the Olympic Peninsula. *Right:* Low-lying fog obscures the timbered canyon walls of the Elwha River, which flows for some 40 miles from the Olympic Mountains to the Strait of Juan de Fuca. *Pages 60 and 61:* Purple blossoms of lupine and creamy-white florets of American bistort (alpine buckwheat) add a show of color to alpine meadow on Hurricane Ridge, some 5,000 feet high in the Olympics.

Yellow monkey flowers bring a touch of brightness to the varied greens of ferns, moss and lichen in an Olympic rain forest. *Left:* Wilderness trails along the forested valleys of Olympic National Park lead to regions of pristine beauty, ice-cold streams, hidden lakes and enchanting waterfalls.

Ocean fog frequently sweeps into Olympic forests, creating ghostly
islands of tree tops. *Right:* Pacific trillium, fern and bleeding heart or
Dutchman's Breeches grow at the base of a giant cedar along Boones Creek
in Olympic National Park.

Ediz Hook is a long, curving sandspit extending into the Strait of Juan de Fuca and providing protection for the busy harbor of Port Angeles. *Left: Nine-mile-long Lake Crescent lies below Mount Storm King in a deep basin scoured out by ancient glaciers. Pages 68-69:* The Strait of Juan de Fuca, viewed from a ridge high on the north side of the Olympics, was named for a legendary explorer who claimed to have sailed these waters in 1592.

Deerfoot or vanilla leaf with its dainty white blossoms is one of the lovely
shade-tolerant plants found in Olympic peninsula forests. When dried, the
leaves have the sweet scent of vanilla. *Right:* Pacific Dogwoods flower
profusely in springtime, very much at home in shady forests of evergreens and
along the banks of streams. *Pages 72 and 73:* Fallen tree serves as nurse log for a
seedling tree; in the forests, decaying logs replenish the soil and nourish
seedlings until their roots grow into the ground.

Fishing boats and floats cast colorful reflections in the water at Port Townsend. *Left:* Hemlock branches form a lovely backdrop for foxglove, which flourishes in Northwest meadows, woods and gardens. *Pages 76 and 77:* Sequim Bay and Discovery Bay can be seen in this northeasterly view over forested slopes and misty cloud bands from Hurricane Ridge in the Olympics.

Commencement Bay, named by the Wilkes Expedition of 1841, is the
deep-water harbor of Tacoma, a busy center for wood, chemical and industrial
products and international shipping. *Left.* Starrett House is one of the many
well-maintained Victorian era homes in Port Townsend, which was port
of entry to Puget Sound and the busiest trade center in the Northwest
during the 19th century.

The ice-clad cone of 14,410-foot Mount Rainier seems to rest on a blanket of clouds in this view towards the southeast from Tolmie Peak. *Right:* Gig Harbor is a quiet haven for commercial fishing vessels, sailboats and sports craft, protected from gales by the surrounding hills. It was named in 1841 by the Wilkes Expedition, when crew members in the ship's gig found shelter here from a storm on Puget Sound.

The skyline of downtown Seattle, named for the great Indian chief, is viewed across Elliott Bay, named in honor of Reverend J. L. Elliott, chaplain with the Wilkes Expedition of 1841. *Left:* Fishing nets and floats form a decorative pattern at Seattle's fishing harbor. *Pages 84 and 85:* Rows of new corn grow in the fertile bottom land of Samish Valley, named for one of the Indian tribes which lived on the San Juans and the nearby coastal plains.

Foxgloves bloom in red and white along Nooksack River Canyon in the shadow of Mount Baker. *Right:* In this double image, a cityscape of Seattle is seen through the pink blossoms of rhododendron, the state flower of Washington; the Space Needle stands at right center. *Pages 88 and 89:* Winter sun and sky are reflected in the Skagit River which flows between forests, logged-over lands and farms rich with alluvial soil, past Mount Vernon to the waters at the northern edge of Puget Sound.

This calm sailing scene is at slack tide in Deception Pass, a deep, rock-walled chasm between Whidbey and Fidalgo Islands, through which the waters surge with violent power at ebb tides and dramatic force on returning floods. *Left:* Weathered root stands on the pebbled beach of Samish Head, near Edison on the coast east of the northern San Juans. *Pages 92 and 93:* Weather-beaten, moss-covered picket fence outlines a section of English Camp National Historical Site on San Juan Island.

Sucia Island is one of the northernmost of the San Juans, lying in the Strait of Georgia. Fossilized specimens of a tiny prehistoric horse were once found in a clay deposit here. *Left:* Rosy-fingered dawn is reflected in the water of the harbor at La Conner, a picturesque fishing village at the northern reaches of Puget Sound; Mount Baker and the Cascade Range are seen in the distance.

The Strait of Juan de Fuca reaches toward the ocean in this view across a golden field of grass accented with red of thistle on a southern height of San Juan Island. *Right:* Ice-capped Mount Baker rises in the background above gulls on pilings at the Anacortes ferry landing on Fidalgo Island. Settlers in 1860 first called the town Ship Harbor; Amos Bowman, who bought the site in 1876, gave it the maiden name of his wife—Anna Curtis—but changed the spelling to make it sound as Spanish as the name of the island.

Below: Marguerite daisies and horsetails are unusual companions in the close-up on Orcas Island, which was named not for the killer whales in the San Juan waters, but for a Spanish viceroy in 18th century Mexico. *Left:* Lime Kiln lighthouse on the west central shore of San Juan Island gives warning to ships sailing in Haro Strait. *Pages 100 and 101:* Lopez Island and Rosario Strait are seen in the golden glow of the setting sun from Mount Erie on Fidalgo Island.

Summer grasses, Queen Anne's Lace and a clump of pink-blossomed thistle are detailed on Orcas Island. *Right:* Tilted strata in the rock formations of the San Juan Islands are frequently seen as are the blue waters, blue skies, white peaks of the Cascades and the gleaming ice dome of Mount Baker. *Pages 104 and 105:* Reddish trunks and green foliage of madrona trees (or Pacific madrone) frame the west bay of Sucia Island.

Golden mist at sunrise silhouettes tall evergreens at American Camp National Historical Site on San Juan Island. *Right:* The expanse of Haro Strait is viewed to the west from Young Hill on San Juan Island. *Pages 108 and 109:* Mount Constitution, 2,454-feet, on Orcas Island was named by the Wilkes Expedition of 1841 in honor of the U.S. Navy frigate *Constitution* whose resistance to British shot during the War of 1812 earned it the popular name, *Old Ironsides.*

The vivid sunset draws a golden line across surface of Haro Strait which is a
major ship channel between Vancouver Island, British Columbia and San Juan
Island, where this photograph was made. *Left:* The distinctive madrona tree,
which continually sheds and renews its bark, is designated *Arbutus Menziesii* in
honor of Archibald Menzies, surgeon and botanist with the Vancouver
expedition of 1792, who noted its frequent appearance in coastal forests and
along the shores of Hood Canal, Puget Sound and the San Juan Islands.

Brown algae number in the hundreds, ranging from feathery filamented species less than a foot long to great kelp over 100 feet in length, and can be found growing from low-tide mark (as these were at Cape Flattery) to ocean depths of 100 feet or more.

You are never quite alone when you walk the western reaches of Washington State: the ghosts of history sail the waters of the varied shore, the ocean, straits and sound; the spirits of legend come to life throughout the rugged land, the rocks, capes and islands. And the waves, rivers and forests speak in a multitude of voices, whispers, murmurs and roars.

"The coast from Cape Disappointment to Cape Flattery," wrote James Swan in 1857, "is nearly north and south, and can be traveled almost the entire length on a beautiful sand-beach, with the exceptions of the openings of Shoal-water Bay, Gray's Harbor, the Copalis, Queniult, and one or two other small rivers. Only a few points jutting into the sea render a portage over them necessary, but the whole distance is easily traversed with the occasional aid of a canoe."

But you do not get to know a land by ever-moving in a straight line. Here on the Washington shores, the ages, waters and forces of nature have created a thousand turnings and diversions for those susceptible to the temptation of mysterious, inviting byways and to the innocence of the Blakean vision "To see a World in a Grain of Sand/And Heaven in a Wild Flower."

As the Raven flies, it is true, the distance of Washington's Pacific shore is less than 160 miles, but the salt waters of the sea wash a tidal shoreline extending over 3000 miles. The Washington shoreline of the Strait of Juan de Fuca is almost 180 miles. Hood Canal moves inland some 60 miles, but it has a shoreline of over 240 miles. And Puget Sound presents a shoreline of 1800 miles. You travel from the Columbia River to Cape Flattery, thence to Admiralty Inlet and along the shores of canal, peninsula and islands of San Juan, and from Budd Inlet, and Commencement Bay to the Strait of Georgia. And along the way there are headlands to climb, dunes to slide, bays to travel, forest trails to take, river banks to follow, jutting points to circle, tide pools to study, harbors to visit, inlets and coves to search, meadows to cross, marshlands to wade, beaches to comb, lakes to find, piers and docks and logs to walk plus a multitude of islands to explore. Though the heavy hand of man has cut and cleared and altered the face of the land, the shores continue as never-ending, ever-changing regions of beauty awaiting your discovery and making you kin to the first adventuresome natives and early explorers.

For countless centuries these shores knew only the tribal peoples, the Coast Indians, sometimes called the Canoe Peoples, who lived, traveled, traded and sometimes, warred along the waterways. Their first visitors may have been Chinese voyagers during the middle of the fifth century. In books compiled during the Liang Dynasty of the sixth century, court historians wrote of a Buddhist monk named Hui shen who spoke of sailing to the Wonderful Land of Fusang that lay 20,000 li, or about 7,000 miles, to the east of China. In his account, Hui shen said that in the second year of the Sung dynasty (A.D. 458) five monks came to this country. Some scholars speculate that the monks sailed or drifted along Russian shores past Kamchatka, across to Alaska and down the Pacific Coast to the shores of Baja California, then traveled into Mexico and New Mexico. Such a voyage would have been possible at that time because the Chinese were skilled seamen with many generations of experience sailing the seas to the south and to the west in massive junks with crews of several hundred men.

A present-day Chinese maritime historian cites the recent discovery off the Santa Barbara coast of an ancient tool-worked stone as evidence of early Chinese voyages to the California coast. This stone is similar to those once used for cleaning seaweed from the anchor chains of seagoing junks. Although Hui shen gave accurate details of the beginning of his voyage and of the land and peoples of Fusang, he made no mention of landings along the Northwest coast. Such landings may well have been made, if for no other reason than to replenish supplies of fresh water. Where, is impossible to tell and legends of the Northwest Indians gave no hint.

There is a tale told in the last century, by an old Indian who had heard of a strange people on a strange craft which had come ashore near Cape Flattery. This was long before the time of his father's father, over a hundred years before the visit of Juan de Fuca. The description of the large vessel, as handed down by the Indians, was that of a Japanese junk. The Indians did not kill the crew members from the wrecked vessel, but kept them as slaves. Many were skilled craftsmen and taught the Indians how to build the canoes which they were to use for several hundred years. It was told that these slaves were sold to other tribes along the coast, and the price was very high, particularly for the canoe builders.

In 1895, J. A. Costello wrote: "As a craft of extreme graceful lines combined with great utility there are none which compare with this canoe. In the hands of the skillful native it can brave the fierce tempests which sweep along the northwest coast of our continent, with the ease and buoyancy of an aquatic bird. It is true that nature has lent assistance in furnishing a wood (cedar) that for lightness and facility for working cannot be excelled the world over, but the art of the native in fashioning this craft is far in advance of all his other attainments.

"So perfect are all its lines for swift sailing, so adapted as a carrier are its dimensions, that McKay, the designer of the clipper-vessel, the ocean greyhound of the earlier part of this century, copied his model after this canoe."

Though the shipwrecked Japanese craftsmen may have been legendary, a crew of Chinese carpenters, shipbuilders and seamen from Canton and Macao voyaged across the Pacific in 1788 with English sea captain John Meares. Meares established a fur trading post at Nootka Sound on Vancouver Island, north across the Strait of Juan de Fuca from the Washington shore. The Chinese craftsmen not only built the fort and village, but also constructed a seagoing schooner.

Floats are colorful reminders of the more than a century-old Northwest fishing industry, which now includes many unique aquaculture operations or "salmon farms."

In 1857 James Swan wrote: "The hats of the Queniult and other Northern Indians are made of precisely the same conical form as the Chinese hats, and are only worn in wet weather to shed rain. This peculiar form has either been handed down to them by tradition, or was introduced among them by the Chinese who were carried to Nootka by Meares from Canton in 1788, to assist in building the schooner Northwest America, and who, remained with the Indians, and took wives among them."

While the schooner was being built, Meares sailed down the coast. He knew of the charts of the Spanish explorer Bruno Heceta who, in August 1775, had discovered a bay which gave indications of a large river. Heceta had named the river *Rio de San Roque,* the bay *Bahia de la Asuncion,* and the cape *Cabo San Roque.* In the course of his search Meares came upon a point of land and a body of water which he called Cape Shoal-water and Shoal-water Bay. This was on July 5, 1788. In his journal he wrote: "It was our wish to have sent the long-boat to sound near the shoals, in order to discover if there was any channel, but the weather was so cloudy, and altogether had so unsettled an appearance, that we were discouraged from executing such a design. Nothing, therefore, was left to us but to coast it along the shore and endeavor to find some place where the ship might be brought to a secure anchorage. On the morning of the sixth, the wind blew from the north, with a strong heavy sea. At half past ten, being within three leagues of Cape Shoal-water, we had a perfect view of it, and with the glasses we traced the line of coast to the southward, which presented no opening that promised any thing like a harbor. A high, bluff promontory bore off us southeast at the distance of only four leagues, for which we steered to double, with the hope that between it and Cape Shoal-water we should find some sort of a harbor."

Meares concluded: "We can now with safety assert that there is no such river as that of St. Roc exists, as laid down in the Spanish charts." Meares changed the name of the rocky promontory from San Roque to Cape Disappointment and the bay to Deception Bay. But it was for him, as

Meares wrote: "...a day very unfavorable to the business of making discoveries," because he was at that time in the mouth of the river named Columbia in 1792 by Captain Robert Gray who is credited with its discovery.

Gray had made an earlier voyage, leaving Boston with trade goods to exchange for furs from the Indians. He reached the Pacific coast in 1788 and as he sailed north noticed signs of a large river. Sea conditions were too rough to permit entry and Gray headed on to Nootka. After a year of accumulating a cargo of furs at Nootka, Gray sailed to China, where he sold the furs and purchased tea and other Oriental commodities. He returned to Boston by way of Africa and the Atlantic. He managed to obtain backers for a second trading expedition to the Northwest Coast and returned to Nootka in the summer of 1791, collecting furs from fall to early spring of the next year.

In April 1792 Gray decided to search once again for the river and was sailing south off the western shore of the Olympic Peninsula when he met with the northbound English ship *Discovery,* commanded by Captain George Vancouver. Vancouver described this meeting in his journal: "At four o'clock a sail was discovered to the westward standing in shore. This was a great novelty, not having seen any vessel but our consort during the last eight months. She soon hoisted American colours, and fired a gun to leeward. At six we spoke to her. She proved to be the ship *Columbia,* commanded by Mr. Robert Gray, belonging to Boston, whence she had been absent nine months...."

Gray told Vancouver of his belief that a great river lay to the south. Vancouver, who

Anemone and starfish share one of many tidal pools which form outdoor aquariums of marine creatures with each low tide.

had just sailed these coastal waters, had found no signs of the legendary Great River of the West and had written in his journal: "..we could not possibly have passed any safe navigable opening, harbour or place of security for shipping on this coast."

Gray continued south on his search and on May 11, 1792, saw dark and muddy water coming out from the shore. This convinced him that he had found the entrance to his river and he gave orders to sail across the bar. He came into a broad freshwater flow where his ship was soon encircled by many canoes. Gray found the Indians receptive to trading furs for trinkets and stayed several days. He went upstream a short distance, returned to the mouth for a few more days of trading, then sailed north again to Nootka. There, he told the Spanish captain Juan Francisco de la Bodega y Quadra of his discovery of the Columbia River and drew charts of its location.

Subsequently, Bodega y Quadra told Vancouver of Gray's discovery of the great river. In October 1792, Vancouver gave orders to Lieutenant W. R. Broughton of his expedition to survey the Columbia. Broughton traveled upstream about 100 miles according to his reckoning, near to the area now called the Columbia Gorge. He named Mount Hood in Oregon for then admiral of the British navy Samuel Hood and Point Vancouver, for his commander. The bay near the mouth of the Columbia, called *Asuncion* by Heceta and *Deception* by Meares, was renamed by Broughton *Baker's Bay,* in honor of the captain of the American schooner, *Jenny,* which he found anchored there.

This is the bay which the Lewis and Clark expedition called "Haley's Bay for a favorite trader with the Indians." The explorers were approaching the bay in November 1805 and recorded in their journals that there was "Great joy in camp. We are in view of the ocean, this great Pacific Ocean which we have been so long anxious to see, and the roaring or noise made by the waves breaking on the rocky shores may be heard distinctly."

Conditions were not entirely pleasant for the members of the expedition and Clark's journal entry for November 15 stated: "The rainy weather continued without a longer intermission than two hours at a time...the most disagreeable time I have experienced, confined on a tempest coast, wet. In this situation we have been for six days past. Fortunately the wind lay about three o'clock. We loaded in great haste and set out, passed the blustering point, below which is a sand beach...The immense swells from the main ocean, immediately in front of us, raised to such a height that I concluded to form a camp on the highest spot I could find in the marshy bottom and proceed no further by water...The ocean is immediately in front of us and gives us an extensive view of it from Cape Disappointment to Point Adams." (Point Adams lies south across the Columbia River on the Oregon shore.)

In about 1855, James Swan was near the site of the Lewis and Clark camp, when he wrote of his trip from Shoalwater Bay to watch the salmon fishing on the Columbia. "As we approached Chenook Point, the tide had fallen enough to enable us to walk on firmer sand...Looking up the river, almost in a line due east, Mount St. Helen's reared its snowy head high in the region of the clouds. The rapidly increasing morning rendered it distinctly visible, although a hundred miles in the interior."

Lewis and Clark had been a few miles upstream when they caught sight of Mount St. Helens and had noted: "...we had a full view of the mountain...it rises in the form of a sugar loaf to a great height, and is covered with snow.

Chinook Point, at the eastern edge of Baker Bay, was named for the once-powerful Indian peoples of this region. It was they who greeted Captain Gray on his entry into the Columbia. The Clark journal noted: "This Chinook nation is about 400 souls; inhabit the country on the small rivers which run into the bay below us and on the ponds to the northwest of us, live principally on fish and roots. They are well armed with fusees and sometimes kill elk, deer and fowl."

The Chinook had long been known for their ability as traders and their language was the main basis for the Chinook jargon which became the trade language and primary means of communication between whites and Indians throughout the Northwest. Theodore Winthrop wrote in 1353: "A grotesque jargon called Chinook is the lingua-franca of the Whites and Indians of the Northwest. It is a jargon of English, French, Spanish, Chinook, Kallapooga, Haida, and other tongues, civilized and savage. It is an attempt on a small scale to nullify Babel by combining a confusion of tongues into a confounding of tongues..."

Many of the words continue to color Northwest language such as: tyee meaning chief or big boss; skookum for strong or powerful; potlatch, both a gift and to give; and tillicum for people or tribe. Today, when winter cold has its grip on the region and ice and snow make travel difficult, even for a few days, people express their wish for a chinook. This is a very special Pacific wind which overnight can melt the largest icicles and crusted banks of snow.

In 1895 Joseph Costello wrote: "Intimately associated with legend and folk lore of the Indians of Puget Sound is the south wind, the balmy Chinook, the harbinger, the first breath of early spring time. It is the precursor of all that is glorious in pleasant days, sunshine and joy. It comes up over the land, perfumed and odorous from the sea islands. It's touch is like that of a maiden's palm, gentle and soft. Its tread is silent like the flight of a peri, but it is strong in its coming, for snow peaks and icy crags melt before it like banks of fog. It may come in May or it may come in December, and its influence is felt for good. The Indians watch for its coming as they did for the salmon, the king of fishes, long before the white man came upon the coast to share in its benign influence."

And one of the world's great species of fish commemorates the tribe with the name Chinook salmon.

On the west side of Baker Bay, not far from the Lewis and Clark campsite, is Ilwaco, named for Elowahka Jim, son-in-law of the tribal leader, Chief Comcomly. The town, just inside the mouth of the Columbia, is protected from Pacific storms by the tall headlands that stand to the west. During salmon season, the harbor is one of the busiest in the Northwest with hundreds of charter and private boats heading out to sea for chinook, silver, tuna and various types of cod and flounder.

To the south and west of Ilwaco are the headlands which Meares named Cape Disappointment, and which encompass McKenzie Head and North Head.

On the tip of Cape Disappointment the new Lewis and Clark Interpretive Center now stands near the few reminders of Fort Canby which had been built in 1864. Fort Canby State Park covers 1666 acres between Cape Disappointment Lighthouse and North Head Lighthouse. The explorers were near the site of the future fort when they eyed the ocean and bar in 1805. Clark took note of what is now called North Head and wrote that he named it Point Lewis "after my particular friend." The continuing and violent power of the seas prompted a later journal entry referring to "the Great Western Ocean, I can't say Pacific, as since I have seen it, it has been the reverse."

Man-made jetties now provide some protection and control of the waters of the Columbia bar, but the shores below Cape Disappointment Lighthouse were long known as the "Graveyard of the Pacific." More than 170 shipwrecks have been recorded at the bar.

Olympic National Park is wilderness home for blacktail deer, Roosevelt elk, black bear, cougar, mountain goats, marmot, bobcat and numerous other species of mammals.

Navy Lieutenant Charles Wilkes, commander of the U.S. Expedition of 1841, wrote of the entrance to the Columbia River: "Mere description can give little idea of the terrors of the bar. All who have seen it have spoken of the wildness of the scene and the incessant roar of the waters, representing it as one of the most fearful sights that can possibly meet the eye."

On July 17, 1841, one of Wilkes' ships, *Peacock*, under the command of Lieutenant William Hudson, went aground west of Cape Disappointment. Peacock Spit was named for this ship. After construction of the north jetty, sand filled in behind to form a beach.

The headlands provide excellent vantage points for watching winter storms on the ocean. And when the weather is clear, the long expanse of the coastal shore extends northward before you.

In April 1792, while about two leagues offshore from Cape Disappointment, Vancouver noted: "The country now before us presented a most luxuriant landscape, and was probably not a little heightened in beauty by the weather that prevailed. The more interior parts were somewhat elevated, and agreeably diversified with hills, from which it gradually descended to the shore, and terminated in a sandy beach. The whole had the appearance of a continued forest, extending north as far as the eye could reach, which made me very solicitous to find a port

California poppies brighten field on one of the tide-washed San Juan Islands north of Puget Sound. The home of tall evergreens, flowering honeysuckle and red currant, lady-slipper orchids and dogtooth violets.

in the vicinity of a country presenting so delightful a prospect of fertility."

Vancouver was viewing the Willapa Hills on the mainland, which rise above the east shore of Meares' Shoal-water Bay, now known as Willapa Bay. The sandy beach he mentions is the broad expanse of North Beach Peninsula which extends from the cape northward to where the ocean joins the tidal waters of the bay. It is more popularly known as Long Beach Peninsula and forms a 28-mile barrier between the ocean and the bay. When the tide goes out, thousands of people come in, to dig the watery shores for razor clams, or to fish the surf for sea perch, occasional flounder and cod. If you enjoy beachcombing, you can travel the distance of the shore in search of treasures from the sea, which include the sought-after glass floats carried by Pacific currents from distant nets of Japanese and Russian fishermen.

Your meanderings along the ocean side of the peninsula will bring you to Leadbetter Point and a view north across the waters to Cape Shoalwater. The point is now a state park of some 770 undeveloped acres. Bird watches have sighted almost 200 varieties of birds here.

Vancouver was offshore in 1792 when he wrote: "... after leaving Cape Disappointment, we made Cape Shoal-water, and endeavoured to enter Shoal-water Bay; but considering, from the appearance of the breakers, that the harbor was inaccessible to the ship, and having a fair wind, we sailed on to the northward."

You, however, will turn southward along the dunes of the point, perhaps finding some wild strawberries or huckleberries and traveling the coves and marshes of the bayshore of the peninsula. There are several small communities around the bay, such as Oysterville and Nahcotta, reminiscent of picturesque New England fishing villages. From 1889 to 1930 there was a narrow-gauge railroad serving the north peninsula between Nahcotta and Ilwaco, a distance of about 15 miles. Departure and arrival times for the train were never the same two days in a row, because the ferries from Astoria and cargo vessels could come into the Ilwaco docks only on high water and the schedule was arranged to make connections at high tide. The train was often called the "Clamshell Railroad" because much of the cargo from the peninsula was clams from Long Beach.

The native peoples of the region had long used the quiet bay and the surrounding countryside as a source of food. Archeologists have studied a site on the peninsula which dates back almost two thousand years. Here, they have found remains of deer, elk, and harbor seal as well as shells from oysters, razor clams, cockles and bones from salmon.

In 1857, James Swan, who had lived by the bay for several years, described some of the fruits and vegetables used by the Indians: "The most pleasant, cooling, and healthy vegetable is the sprout of the wild raspberry. This shoots up with great rapidity, seeming to grow as fast as asparagus. These sprouts are collected in bundles and brought into the lodge, where they are denuded of their tough outer skin, and the centre is as crisp and tender as a cucumber, and being slightly acid, is delicious. They are slightly astringent; and as the herring begin to make their appearance at the same time, and from their oily nature, and the immoderate manner in which the Indians eat them, are apt to produce disorders of the bowels, the sprouts, being freely eaten at the same time, counteract the effect. So with the berry of this plant, which is ripe in June, when the salmon begin to be taken in the Columbia. This fruit, which is called salmon-berry, and is found in the greatest abundance, is also beneficial to counteract any ill effects that might be occasioned by inordinate eating of the rich salmon."

Towering waves, though beautiful to watch, carry the destructive power which breaks down the headlands and continually changes the face of the Pacific shore.

"The salmon-berry just mentioned is the first fruit ripe, and is soon followed by strawberries, great quantities of which are found in the plains of the peninsula, and in all the prairie lands on or near the coast. Then comes the whortleberry, blueberry, and a beautiful coral-red berry like a currant, called red whortleberry, but of a different character. This fruit tastes like and resembles the common red currant, and I think, by cultivation, it would make not only a beautiful and ornamental shrub, but the quantity and quality of the fruit would be improved. Blackberries, gooseberries, and wild black currants next follow, and then comes the salal. This beautiful evergreen shrub may be found varying in height from two feet to ten. The leaf is a dark green, like the laurel; the bark on the smaller limbs and twigs is red, or of a reddish-brown. The flowers are in clusters, like the currant, having from 14 to 21 on one stem. The fruit, when ripe, is a very dark purple, almost black, rough on the outside, very juicy, and of a sweetish, slightly acid taste, and of the size of large buck-shot. It is excellent cooked in any form, and is dried by the Indians, and pressed into cakes containing some five or six pounds, which are covered with leaves and rushes, so as to exclude the air, and then stored in a dry place for winter's use. This plant continues to blossom till late in December in certain areas, although it has but one crop, which is ripe in August.

"The cranberry, which is very plentiful, and forms quite an article of traffic between whites and Indians, is next in season . . ."

Lewis and Clark found wild cranberries when they were in the region in 1805. Along the peninsula there are now several hundred acres of bogs where the bright red berries have been cultivated for market since 1883.

Willapa Bay has been known for its oysters since the 1850s, when the first barrels were shipped to San Francisco. There are processing plants where you can watch the oyster shuckers prepare the oysters for market, rapidly wielding sharp-pointed blades to pry the hard shells open. The beds in the tidal flats are now all privately-owned oyster farms and poaching is against the law.

Willapa National Wildlife Refuge, along the tip of the southern arm of the bay, was established in 1937 and is a favored area for watching and photographing the Canadian geese, Black brants and other migratory wildfowl which travel the Pacific Flyway.

The eastern shore of the bay leads northward across several rivers, among them the Naselle, Nemah and Willapa, through pastoral and sometimes marshy meadowlands, and by the pungent mud flats where the oysters dwell. Although the great forests which Vancouver mentioned have long since been cut, there are new growths and more distant timberlands which continue to sustain lumber production in the area.

On the north shore of the bay is the Shoalwater Indian Reservation and the small village of Tokeland, named for Chief Toke, a tribal leader during the middle of the last century. Sandy beaches lead to North Cove and Cape Shoalwater.

The wind is a frequent and insistent companion as you walk along the ocean shore north towards Point Chehalis and the entrance to Grays Harbor. Clumps of beach grass and the creeping stems of sand verbena seek to hold the fine gray sand of the ever-shifting dunes. And the gnarled shapes of stunted trees above the shoreline form picturesque reminders of the force of Pacific gales. To the north on the harbor

Salmon are the prize sought after by the fleet of commercial and sports fishing boats shown in the protected harbor of Westport.

side of Point Chehalis is Westport, where a protected cove is the home for a fleet of boats used in both commercial and sport fishing for salmon and crab.

The American explorer and fur trader Robert Gray, on his way south in search of the Columbia River, noted his discovery of the harbor in his log for May 7, 1792: "Being within six miles of the land, saw an entrance in the same, which had a very good appearance of a harbor; . . . We soon saw, from our mast head, a passage in between the sand bars. At 5 P.M. came to, in five fathoms water, sandy bottom, in a safe harbor, well sheltered from the sea by long sand bars and spits."

Gray named the bay Bulfinch's Harbor for Charles Bulfinch of Boston, one of the owners of his ship *Columbia*. In October 1792, Joseph Whidbey of the Vancouver expedition surveyed the harbor and noted the name of Gray's Harbor on his charts in honor of the discoverer. The Vancouver charts were published, whereas those of Gray were not, and the name has remained. The Spanish explorers Galiano and Valdez, also in 1792, helped establish the name by charting it "Puerto de Gray."

Among the several rivers flowing into the harbor, the largest is the Chehalis, coming from the western slopes of the Cascades; the Wishkah, Hoquiam and Humptulips drain southward from the Olympics. Aberdeen and Hoquiam are twin cities of the lumber and wood products, fishing and shipping industries on the harbor. Aberdeen is derived from the Scottish, meaning "the meeting of two rivers", which here are the Chehalis and Wishkah. The wife of one of the early settlers in the territory was a native of Aberdeen, Scotland. Hoquiam is supposedly named from the Indian word *Ho-qui-umpts,* meaning hungry for wood, because of the amount of driftwood at the mouth of the river.

In earlier days, sailors and loggers looked upon Aberdeen as a wide-open town, and for a period it lived up to its reputation with a street lined with saloons and resorts sporting names such as Merry Widow, Klondike, and Lone Jack, as well as those of some Ivy League sihools such as The Harvard and The Yale. The lessons were not always pleasureable when the lumberjacks and seamen awoke with their bank rolls gone or at sea on a strange ship.

Today, log rustling is sometimes a problem and the timber companies have registered brands which they put on the ends of their logs. A state-licensed log patrol rides the range, checking on ownership, particularly when the ends of logs have been freshly cut and no brand shows. Patrol members also clear navigation of logs which have floated away from booms, salvaging a million or more board feet a year, and sharing the proceeds with the owners.

The upper shore of the bay leads across the Humptulips, past fishing boats and docks to the towns and resorts north along the ocean beaches.

Meares was on this way north from Cape Disappointment in July 1788 when he noted: "The face of the country assumed a very different appearance. Many beautiful spots covered with the finest verdure solicited our attention, and the land rose in a very gradual ascent to the distant mountains, skirted by a white sandy beach down to the sea. As we sailed along, spacious lawn and hanging woods everywhere met the delighted eye—but not a human being appeared to inhabit the fertile country of New Albion." The region was first called New Albion or New England when Sir Francis Drake sailed northward along the Pacific Coast.

The Moclips River reaches the ocean near the southwest corner of the Quinault Indian Reservation. On July 14, 1775 the schooner *Sonora,* under the command of Francisco de la Bodega y Quadra, was at anchor here. Seven men were sent to shore for fresh water and were killed by the natives. That same day Bodega y Quadra sailed north to join Bruno Heceta, commander of the *Santiago,* who was anchored near present-day Point Grenville, a high promontory reaching into the ocean. Heceta, with members of his staff and crew, went ashore and raised a cross, taking possession of the region for Spain. He named the point Punta de los Martires, or Point of the Martyrs, in memory of the slain men of the *Sonora.* Later Spanish explorers called it Punta de la Bastida, or Point of the Bastion, because of its fortress-like appearance. In April 1792, Vancouver named it Point Grenville in honor of Baron William Grenville, a British statesman.

The point marks the beginning of a changing character for the coastline to the north. Rugged headlands and steep cliffs rise above the tidal shore; the beach becomes narrower, sloping sharply down to the sea. Travel along the shore is hard and sometimes impossible, except at low tide.

Three miles north of Point Grenville is the mouth of the Quinault River and the centuries-old Indian village of Taholah, tribal headquarters for the Quinaults. During the last century, an early settler wrote: "There's a long shingle of beach, a glistening reach of sand, bright under the glare of summer suns, with a broad sweep of salty bay, flecked here and there with a few jagged and black-looking rocks, the sporting ground of the sea otter the year round. Outside the line of pointed rocks the swells of the restless Pacific Ocean come tumbling in and are broken into white foam and dashing spray upon the rocks, or missing those roll on upon the beach and curl the shimmering sand into pretty riffles. At the rear is a dense background of forest that reaches far into the interior until it runs out at the timber line far up the sloping sides of the Olympics. The Quinault River rushes out through the forest past the village and pours its purling waters into the long stretch of bay, as if glad to escape from the imprisonment of woods and jungle.

"The great highway of the tribe, next to the ocean itself, is the swiftly flowing Quinault River, up which they run their light canoes to the lake of the same name. In the summer, and sometimes, too, when the snow whitens the upper lying forests, the canoe highway is relinquished and the Indian takes the trail through the woods or over the mountains. From the lake of Quinault, resting in the foothills of Olympics, within hearing of the ocean's roar, many trails are blazed to camps, made long years ago, where fat elk have been butchered and dried by the Indians.

"The mountains form the summer's paradise of the tribe. It is there that bands of elk may be seen gamboling on the unmelted snow in the glare of the sun; and the black bear may be seen in numbers feeding on the luxurious wild berries. But the lake itself, perhaps, is regarded by the Indians as their gretest natural treasure. The year round it is the haunt of numerous kinds of salmon, tempted there from the ocean to spawn. Thousands of trout may be seen also in its transparent depths and wild fowl flock to its inviting feeding grounds in great numbers from all climes. At times, too, a deer makes its way from bank to bank. It is an ideal spot, but will not much longer be the domain of the Quinault tribe."

Many vacationers come to the resort on the lake, but the domain continues to be that of the Quinaults; after years of negotiations and delays, the reservation treaty was signed in November 1873 by President Grant. Theirs is the largest reservation in the western part of the state, with some 27 miles of coastline, much of which they keep closed to travel by non-Indians. The area contained nearly 100,000 acres of virgin timber, but most of the great wilderness forest of spruce, cedar, hemlock and fir has been logged over, clear-cut by timber companies. The great runs of salmon are diminished because the spawning streams have been clogged with slashings and debris from the logging. Fast-growing alder and vine maple are hiding some of the scars on the land, but there are few signs of new evergreen forests.

The Quinaults are working to clear their land and streams, trying to establish reforestation areas and to develop fish hatcheries. The river continues to carry Indian canoes for special trips to and from the lake and occasional racing events. And at the mouth of the river, cedar logs are sometimes made into dugout canoes, now with the help of a chain saw.

Near the northwest corner of the Quinault Reservation the Queets River completes its journey from Olympic glaciers through a dense rain forest to the cold waters of the sea. The Queets rain forest is a section of the great protected timberlands ranging from the river valleys of the Bogachiel and the Hoh to the Quinault, in the upper reaches near the lake. Warm, moisture-laden winds from the Pacific cool quickly as they move up the western slopes of the Olympic mountains, releasing snow on the peaks and rain over the forests and meadow-like prairies. The abundance of rainfall, from 100 inches a year to 175 inches in some areas, and the mild temperatures from the warm Japanese current offshore create a humid climate of growth. Myriad varieties of moss and fern carpet the deep humus of the forest floor and cover the trunks of fallen trees, sharing space with the seedlings of shade-tolerant spruce and hemlock. Moss hangs in bearded masses from many shrubs and trees; aerial plants anchor themselves to branches and draw moisture and nutrients from the falling rain. Elderberry and vine maple seek to establish themselves in the shadow of alder and bigleaf maple. Towering above are the great Sitka spruce and hemlock, and where there is more sunlight, Douglas fir and cedar.

In 1909 President Theodore Roosevelt, for whom the Roosevelt elk of the Olympics is named, proclaimed some 600,000 acres of the Olympic forest as Mount Olympus National Monument. In 1938 President Franklin Roosevelt signed the congressional act which established the national park, including the monument, and gave him power to increase the area to almost 900,000 acres. In 1940 he signed the order making the additional acreage part of the park. Now included in the national park are 50 miles of coastline, from north of the mouth of the Queets to just above Cape Alava.

The Olympics were first noted in 1774 by Juan Perez as he sailed along the coast. The mountain he called Sierra de Santa Rosalia was given its classical name of Mount Olympus by John Meares in 1788.

The Vancouver flotilla was nearing the Olympic Park section of the coast on April 28, 1792 when Archibald Menzies, surgeon and botanist of the expedition, entered into his journal: "Early in the morning we had heavy rain and easterly wind with which we edged in for the shore & bore up about 6 or 7 leagues to the Northward ... The land here is low and thickly covered with wood close down to the brink of a steep cliffy shore which appeared pretty straight with a number of elevated rocks scattered along it but laying at no great distance from it; the land further back rose pretty high and mountainous towards the summit of which we observed several patches of snow. Tho' the country here was by no means unpleasant yet there was a sameness in the extent of prospect which soon fatigued the eye and did not afford it that treat of verdant hills interspersed with woods and fertile dales which the Coast more to the Southward presented."

Shell is from one of the tiny shore crabs which like to live among rocks in the water, occasionally scurrying along the sand in search of dead fish. The shell has been discarded after forming a replacement to accommodate its miniscule development.

The prospect along the Olympic shorelines, however, affords a never-ending treat with rocks and reefs and colorful tide pools alive with plants and animals of the sea. Here are the brown, red and green algae, from the great kelp to the sea lettuce, sea moss and plumeria. You can see the barnacles, mussels and limpets anchored to the rocks, holding firmly against the turbulent sea. You can discover the anemone enfolding its green antennae when disturbed, the sea urchin seemingly erecting its red-purple spines, the starfish clinging to a rock with its brown-orange arms, and the tiny hermit crab wearing the shell house it has scavenged along the beach. You can also leave the creatures of the tide pools to live another day; they are important in the chain of life and face enough natural dangers without being forced from their homes to become someone's souvenir.

If you are lucky when combing the beaches, you can find the whole skeleton of a sand dollar, cleaned and whitened by the sand and sea. There are agates, jasper, petrified wood and fossils in the wave-washed gravel along the beaches and at the mouths of rivers. And after a storm, you may find a glass float carried on shore from a distant fishing net.

Menzies' journal for April 28 went on to note: "...at noon...Destruction Island was at the time about three leagues to the Northward of us. It is low and flat, covered only with verdure and engirdled by steep rocky cliffs." Destruction Island was named la Isla de Dolores. Island of Sorrows by Heceta and Bodega y Quadra in 1775, the day before, crewmen were slain near the mouth of the Hoh River. In 1787 Captain Charles Barkley (Barclay in Menzies' journal) of the East Indian Company ship *Imperial Eagle* also lost men at the Hoh River, which he then named Destruction River. Later, the Indian name Hoh was returned to the river and Destruction given to the island.

The six-acre island is about four and one-half miles offshore. Each April it becomes the nesting ground for great numbers of auklets, which make their nests in old tunnels or dig new ones in the earth banks. These burrows help protect the eggs and young hatchlings from the cannibalism of the gulls which also nest on the island. At one time the Hoh Indians would make occasional trips in their canoes to gather gull eggs and some of the auklets for food.

The Hoh Indians, who live on a reservation near the Hoh River may have to resort to the ancient gathering practice if the salmon runs do not increase. The Hohs depend on the salmon for their livelihood and in recent years, both their allowable catch and actual catch have been diminishing. The Indians believe that too many salmon are caught before they can enter the river and the Hohs and the Quinaults have filed suit to reduce ocean fishing by the fleets of commercial trawlers.

James House, one of the elegant Victorian homes built during the 1870s and 80s, when Port Townsend was the most active international harbor on the Pacific Coast.

At a nearby beach you may see fishermen wading into the surf and dragging long-handled nets through the water to gather smelt. Along the coastal shores are headlands, huge rocks and arches to view and, sometimes, to explore. And always, there is the surging power of the seas, awesome both in tempestuous force and tranquil beauty. You can see tree-topped islands, see stacks which were once headlands and the towering rock needles named for the Quileute Indians, or Quillayute; both Anglicized versions of the Indian name which sounds a bit like *kwo-lay-yoot.* You can hike along nearby forests to the Quillayute Reservation, the Quillayute River and the fishing harbor of La Push, the Chinook jargon version of the French fur traders *la bouche,* which means *mouth.*

Quillayute legends tell of help from Raven and how he brought blue-back salmon to the coastal rivers of the Olympic Peninsula. He had been served salmon in the burrow of Mole. Raven found the fish delicious and knew that the people would also like it. He came above ground, hiding scales of the fish in his mouth. As Raven flew away from Mole, he dropped one scale of the salmon into the Quillayute River, one into the Hoh, two into the Queets and the rest into the Quinault. That is why the salmon came to the rivers and why some had more fish than others. Today, there are some who wish that the Raven would once again work his magic.

Near Cape Alava is a unique archeological site where Makah Indian houses dating back 450 years and more were preserved in clay sent down by ancient slides from an adjacent hillside. Slides in the late 1960s revealed artifacts and the presence of the houses. Since then extensive work has been done by University of Washington scientists and the Makahs to unearth and save the rare finds from ancestral homes.

Along the shore of the Peninsula and the Strait of Juan de Fuca there are rocky inlets and coves which offer hidden and treacherous landing sites, used in days long past by marauding bands from northern tribes and during the time of Prohibition by rumrunners. Today, these isolated sites are sometimes used by smugglers of contraband and drugs. On recent occasions, Makah and Coast Guard officials have discovered bales of marijuana washed on shore, cargo lost or jettisoned from a boat or raft pounded by the waves.

"A 19th century settler wrote: "When it comes down to hunting seal or fishing off the coast, the Makah asks nothing better than his stout, roomy cedar canoe. He will chase a whale, too, as quickly as he will a seal. They are great sea rovers and will start off on a three hundred mile voyage in light canoes, down the coast or up the Straits and Sound, with no more serious consideration than if they were going only as far as the nearest bight or inlet."

The Makahs were referred to by an early missionary as the "people who live on a point of land projecting into the sea." They are also known as the Cape people and the reservation of the Makah nation abuts the shores of the Pacific and the Strait of Juan de Fuca at the northwest tip of the Olympic Peninsula where Cape Flattery stands.

Cape Flattery, at the southern entrance to the strait, was named by the English explorer Captain James Cook in March 1778. In his journal he wrote: "Between this island or rock, and the northern extremes of the land, there appeared a small opening which flattered us with the hopes of finding a harbour there. Those hopes lessened as we drew nearer; and at last, we had some reason to think that the opening was closed by low land. On this account I called the point of land to the north of it Cape Flattery." Fog and bad weather prevented Cook

Fisherman's Wharf is home port for Seattle's commercial fishing fleet which sails Pacific waters seeking their limits of salmon, snapper, halibut, sole, cod and crab.

from discovering the strait and he sailed north to a harbor on what is now called Vancouver Island.

One of the members of Cook's staff was Vancouver who contributed so much to the knowledge of the waterways of the strait and the sound with his expedition in 1792.

Menzies, of the Vancouver expedition, described the coast leading to the strait in his journal entry for April 29, 1792: "...we made sail and pursued our course along shore till about noon when we entered the famous Streights of Juan de Fuca. The weather at this time so thick and hazy that we had no observation to determine our latitude. The whole shore we sailed along this forenoon is steep and rocky and entirely lined with a vast number of elevated rocks and islets of different forms and sizes, but the land itself is of a very moderate height covered with pines and stretching back with a very gradual acclivity to form an inland ridge of high mountains in which Mount Olympus claimed a just preeminence...About a Mile or two off this South point of entrance is a flat naked island covered with verdure and faced round with steep rocks, round the North end of which we hauled into the Streights..."

The strait carries the name of a man quoted in a volume, titled *Purchas His Pilgrimes,* published in 1625 by Samuel Purchas, who included material from manuscripts obtained from geographer-writer Richard Hakluyt. One episode told of a British consul, Michael Lok the Elder, who recounted: "When I was at Venice in April, 1596, happly arrived there an old man, about sixty years of age, called commonly Juan de Fuca, but named properly Apostolos Valerianus, of nation a Greek, born in Cephalonia, of profession a mariner, and an ancient pilot of ships." Lok said that de Fuca told him that in 1592 he sailed: "...all along the coast in Nova Spania and California, and the Indies, now called North America, until he came to the latitude 47 degrees; and that, there finding ...a broad inlet of sea, between 47 and 48 degrees of latitude, he entered thereinto, sailing therein more than twenty days, and found that land trended still sometimes northwest, and northeast, and north, and also east southeastward, and very much broader sea than was at the said entrance, and that he passed divers islands in the sailing; and that, at the entrance of this said strait, there is on the northwest coast thereof, a great headland or island, with an exceeding high pinnacle, or spired rock, like a pillar thereupon."

Juan de Fuca and later explorers sought the Strait of Anian, Drake called it the Northwest Passage, a fabled waterway extending through the American continent from the Atlantic to the Pacific, a more direct route from the shores of Europe to the Far East.

The books of Hakluyt and Purchas with their tales of exploration in Western oceans sparked the imagination of many readers. One was Jonathan Swift, who created *Gulliver's Travels*, wherein one of the countries discovered by the hero in 1703 is Brobdingnag. Gulliver's descriptions and map showing the location of this Land of Giants suggest that this may be the Olympic Peninsula. In Gulliver's words: "... I cannot but conclude that our geographers of Europe are in a great error, by supposing nothing but sea between Japan and California; ... and therefore they ought to correct their maps and charts, by joining this vast tract of land to the north-west parts of America, ... The kingdom is a peninsula, terminated to the northeast by a ridge of mountains thirty miles high, which are altogether impassable by reason of the volcanoes upon the tops ... On the other three sides it is bounded by the ocean ... and those parts of the coasts into which the rivers issue are so full of pointed rocks, and the sea generally so rough, that there is no venturing with the smallest of their boats..."

To many, Juan de Fuca is as much a creature of imagination as Gulliver, however, many of his fellow seamen have given him very real recognition. The location of Fuca's Pillar has been variously described by explorers. Meares reported such a rock at the entry to the strait, but called it Pinnacle Rock; Vancouver recorded one near the mainland after passing Tatoosh Island; the Wilkes Expedition of 1841 published a drawing of de Fuca's Pillar; and a member of the U.S. Coast Survey in 1858 mentioned seeing a 75-foot-high column southeast of Tatoosh Island.

Tatoosh Island has been an important reference point at the entrance to the strait since its first lighthouse in 1857, though legend tells that it was not always near Cape Flattery. In times distant, Tatoosh and Destruction Island lived in the ocean near the Hoh River, surrounded by their many children, the rocks of different sizes with which the waves played. After many quarrels, Tatoosh decided to leave her husband. She filled her canoe with her children and traveled up the coast. Her anger continued great and she at last decided that they would probably grow up like their father, whereupon, she threw them out of the canoe at the place now called Point of Arches. Tatoosh continued north to her present home off Cape Flattery in the strait.

Meares is said to have named Tatoosh Island in honor of Chief Tatooche, who had welcomed him when he anchored in the strait. Meares is also credited with assigning the name Juan de Fuca to the strait. In his account of his voyages, Meares wrote that in the summer of 1788: "We had not only traced every part of the coast which unfavorable weather had prevented Captain Cook from approaching, but had also ascertained the real existence of the Strait of John de Fuca, which now renewed its claim to our attention..." Captain William Barkley (Barclay), whose teen-age bride was with him on the voyage, is reported to have put the name of Juan de Fuca on his charts in 1787.

Although the strait is only about a hundred or so miles long (if you measure in a straight line), it has become a highway for ships of the world. From the shores you can watch coastal freighters. container vessels, oil tankers, lumber transports, ferries, ships of the navy and of the fishing fleet. In describing Port Townsend of the 1880s, John Muir wrote: "... all vessels stop here, and they make a lively show about the wharves and in the bay. The winds stir the flags of every civilized nation, while the Indians, in their long-beaked canoes, glide about from ship to ship, satisfying their curiosity or trading with the crews. Keen traders these Indians are, and few indeed of the sailors or merchants from any country ever get the better of them in bargains. Curious groups of people may often be seen, English, French, Spanish, Portuguese, Scancinavians, Germans, Greeks, Moors, Japanese, and Chinese of every rank and station and style of dress and behaviour; settlers from many a nook and bay and island up and down the coast; hunters from the wilderness; tourists on their way home by the Sound and the Columbia River or to Alaska or California."

Along the shore you will travel from bay to bay, on rocky beaches and sandy beaches, over lookout points and occasional arms of land reaching into the strait. You will cross creeks and rivers bearing Indian names, such as Hoko, for a Clallam village; Pysht, for *fish* in the Chinook jargon; and Elwha, for *elk*. You will walk near growths of new trees, logged-over lands and old skid roads on which forest giants were pulled to the water. It was along these tidal shores that Meares in 1788 and Vancouver in 1792 replaced broken spars with tall fir cut from the Olympic Peninsula forest. Timber, lumber and wood products continue to be important in the economy of the region, and you will see sawmills, pulp and paper mills and logs dumped into bays and formed into rafts. And from time to time you will view distant mountains as did Vancouver, who wrote: "The high distant land formed, as already observed, like detached islands, amongst which the lofty mountain, discovered in the afternoon by the third lieutenant (Joseph Baker) and in compliment to him called Mount Baker, rose a very conspicuous object."

Downtown office buildings provide a background for tugs in Seattle harbor, an international waterfront in center of city.

Brightly colored floats can often be seen bobbing on the waves, marking the location of submerged traps utilized to lure the delicately-flavored Dungeness crustacean.

Near the entrance of the strait, in the lee of the eroded headlands of Cape Flattery, is Neah Bay, headquarters village of the Makah peoples. For countless years the Makahs had set out from here on their hunts for seal and whale and fish. Today the harbor continues as a fishing center for both whites and Indians who head out in commercial boats in search of salmon, halibut and cod. Though somewhat protected, the bay still feels the force of winter storms.

To the east are Sekiu and its log rafts and Clallam Bay named for the Indians who called themselves the "strong people" and who the Makahs called the "clam people." Farther on there are the remains of once-busy logging communities, middens with bones and shells from long past meals in ancient Indian villages, and parks for present-day vacationers. And there is Ediz Hook, a four-mile-long sand spit, curving into the strait and protecting the harbor of Port Angeles. Ediz, meaning "good place," was adapted from that of a Clallam Indian village which was once there. On August 2, 1791 Juan Francisco de Eliza anchored in the harbor and named it *Porto de Nuestra Senora de Los Angeles,* because it was the festival day of the Senora. In 1792 Galiano and Valdes shortened it to *Porto de Los Angeles* and that same year Vancouver further abbreviated it to Port Angeles.

In writing of his visit to the Olympic Peninsula in 1889, John Muir wrote: "... in these Washington wilds, living alone, all sorts of men may perchance be found — poets, philosophers, and even fullblown transcendentalists...". At times, however, they did not always live alone, but tried to establish utopian communities. Just east of the Port Angeles townsite, a group headed by George Venable Smith established the Puget Sound Cooperative Colony in 1887. There was to be common ownership of the land and no taxes or rents. Women were to be emancipated from "the slavery of domestic drudgery"; wives who wished to work outside their homes would have household chores done by hired housekeepers. There were to be "free water, free lights and free libraries." The colony flourished for a couple of years, then the leaders began to exchange accusations of fraud and the Utopian dream became lost in the reality of financial receivership.

Port Angeles, however, continues to thrive as harbor, wood products center and waypoint for vacationers.

In his April 30, 1792 journal entry Menzies wrote: "We were not above 18 leagues from the entrance, when the Streights widened out to 9 or 10 leagues across, we however continued our course along the southern shore and in the evening went round the point of a low sandy spit which jutted out from it in very shallow water, when we came to an anchor on the east side of it in 14 fathoms fine black sand about half a mile from the spit which appeared a long ridge of sand strewed over with a good deal of drift wood..."

And Vancouver noted: "The low sandy point of land, which from its great resemblance to Dungeness in the British channel, I called New Dungeness."

This is not the only area where you can find *Cancer magister,* which the textbooks refer to as the common edible crab of the Pacific Coast. The waters of the Northwest, however, seem to have given it a most uncommon delicacy of texture and flavor, and from San Francisco wharves to Alaskan bays, it is most popularly known as Dungeness crab. You may want to try your hand at netting a few in the bay or watch as the metal crab pots are off-loaded from commercial boats just in from coastal waters.

The force of the tides and currents is strong off Dungeness and during the days

Anemones are hardy creatures, sometimes covering the surfaces of rocks in shallow water and under favorable conditions, living as long as 50 years. The green coloring of anemones comes from the effect of sunlight on the chlorophyll-bearing algae which live in their columns and tentacles.

of iron men and wooden ships the settlers would light fires on the beach during stormy weather to give warning to the lookouts on the sailing vessels.

As he headed eastward Vancouver noted: "...our attention was immediately called to a landscape almost as enchantingly beautiful as the most elegant finished pleasure-grounds in Europe. The country presented nearly a horizontal surface, interspersed with some inequalities of ground, which produced a beautiful variety of extensive lawn, covered with luxuriant grass, and diversified with an abundance of flowers. While we stopped to contemplate these several beauties of nature in a prospect no less pleasing than unexpected, we gathered some gooseberries and roses in a considerable state of forwardness."

The region he was viewing has become one of farmlands and cultivated fields in the northern shadow of Mount Olympus. While most of the Olympic Peninsula has more than abundant rainfall, the area around Sequim averages only 16 or so inches a year. Because of the limited precipitation, many farms must be irrigated.

It was on the Manis farm near Sequim that bones of a mastodon were unearthed in 1977. Archeologists discovered a rib with a spear point embedded in it, indicating that hunting peoples were living in the region some 12,000 years ago. Again, in 1980, just a few feet from the original find, the skeletal remains of another Ice Age elephant were discovered. Parallel scratches on some of the bones seem to have been made by stone knives used in cutting away the flesh.

The bones were found in what are called kettle lakes, formed by melting ice masses which blocked the Strait of Juan de Fuca and Puget Sound some 14,000 years ago.

Indian legends tell of a great flood which came at the end of a long winter, when waters from the sky had covered the land and risen over the great mountains, and in the great cold had turned to ice. Shells of clams and oysters and bones of fish, deer and bear had floated on the water and had remained on the sides of the mountains as the ice began to melt. This is why signs of the sea can still be found high on the mountains and why the mountain tops are covered with snow and ice.

To the east of the entry to Sequim Bay, Vancouver came upon an island which he named Protection Island. Two years earlier, in 1790, Quimper had named it Isla de Carrasco, after his second pilot who had discovered it. Menzies later described the view from the summit: "To the north and north west ward the eye roved over a wide expanse of water which seemed to penetrate the distant land through various openings and windings, but a little to the south east of us appeared an inlet which promised fair for affording good shelter for the vessels — Its entrance presents a prospect truly inviting with gentle rising banks on both sides covered with fine verdure and tufted with tall trees loosely scattered..."

This was Discovery Bay which Vancouver named after his ship. Menzies wrote of walking along the "pebbly beach" and finding a sandy point (Carr Point) with a "run of fresh water." "Here we kindled a fire and regaled ourselves with some refreshment, after which we returned on board where we arrived about midnight each well satisfied with the success and pleasure of this day's excursion."

All was not pleasant, however, for Menzies also noted: "In going into the harbour one of the gentlemen shot a small animal which diffused through the air a most disagreeable and offensive smell...I took it to be the Skunk or Polecat."

The east shore of the bay leads around Quimper Peninsula, named for the Spanish explorer, to Port Townsend which Vancouver described as "a very safe and more capacious harbour than Port Discovery; and rendered more pleasant by the high land being at a greater distance from the water-side...To this port I gave the name of Port Townshend, in honor of the noble Marquis of that name."

Walking in sections of Port Townsend — the h in the Port's name was dropped many years ago — is like taking a stroll in the last century; there are elegant Victorian mansions with elaborate roofs, dormers, cupolas and stained glass windows, all beautifully maintained and restored.

To the eastward is Admiralty Inlet which joins the tidal waters of the Strait of Juan de Fuca and Puget Sound. Vancouver named the inlet for the British Board of Admiralty.

In his journal entry, Menzies wrote: "We cannot quit Admiralty Inlet without observing that its beautiful canals and wandering navigable branches traverse through a low flat country upwards of 20 leagues to the southward of its entrance and 8 or 9 leagues to the eastward and to the north east, thus diffusing utility and ornament to a rich country by affording a commodious and ready communication through every part of it, to the termination of the most distant branches. Its short distance from the ocean which is not above 26 leagues, and easy access by the streights of Juan de Fuca is likewise much in its favour should its fertile banks be hereafter settled by any civilized nation."

Of one of the branches Vancouver wrote in May 1792: "Early on Sunday morning, the 13th, we again embarked; directing our route down the inlet, which, after the Right Honorable Lord Hood, I called Hood's Channel." One of his lieutenants entered *canal* on the charts instead of channel and in 1905, the U.S. Geographical Board dropped the *'s*.

Washington State ferry approaches landing at Orcas Island, largest of the San Juans, which offers vacationers many resorts, a state camping park, fishing, swimming and hiking. The ferry system offers sea cruises on routes through waters of San Juans, Puget Sound and Strait of Juan de Fuca.

As you travel along the shores, with its inlets, tide flats, quiet waters and beaches, you will understand the inspiration for the song *Acres of Clams*. There are clams to dig and oysters to rake and in deeper water, fish to take. You will cross rivers with Indian names; Dosewallips, Duckabush, Hamma Hamma and the forks of the Skohomish. There are old logging roads to walk and wooded trails to follow. And there are salmonberries, thimbleberries, elderberries, huckleberries and salal to pick when ready, and once in a while, wild blackberry.

Menzies wrote: "We also met here pretty frequent in the wood with that beautiful native of the Levant the purple Rhododendron, together with the great flowered Dogwood..." There were many "shrubs and underwood" which were new to him: one he named *Arbutus glauca* which is now known as *Arbutus Menziesii* in his honor. This is the madrone which reaches heights of 100 feet or more and whose dark green leaves, pinkish flowers, orange-red fruit and reddish-brown bark give it a distinctive appearance in Northwest coastal forests and lowlands. Dogwoods and rhododendrons continue to thrive in the woods, along the waterways and in plantings in parks and private homes. *Rhododendron macrophyllum,* now the state flower of Washington, can be seen in all its pink-flowered, broad green-leaved beauty in great profusion on the Olympic Peninsula, Hood Canal and Kitsap Peninsula.

Vancouver was near Marrowstone Point when he noted: "To describe the beauties of this region, will, on some future occasion, be a very grateful task to the pen of a skilful panegyrist. The serenity of the climate, the innumerable pleasing landscapes, and the abundant fertility that unassisted nature puts forth, require only to be enriched by the industry of man with villages, mansions, cottages, and other building to render it the most lovely country that can be imagined; whilst the labour of the inhabitants would be amply rewarded, in the bounties which nature seems ready to bestow on cultivation."

Past the salmon hatchery at Hoodsport the canal comes to its southernmost point, curves northeasterly for a short distance, where the western shore of the canal joins the eastern shore of Kitsap peninsula.

The peninsula shows much of "the industry of man" mentioned by Vancouver, in towns both old and new. There are once-flourishing logging and sawmill communities which are now resort and recreation centers, some still with buildings and mansions reminiscent of their historic New England antecedents. Fishing villages that were known for great commercial catches continue with their fishing docks and moorages, now used mainly by sports fishermen and vacationers. There are gardens and farms and tree nurseries raising a million or more Douglas fir seedlings a year. And there are shipyards, such as Bremerton, which have repaired naval vessels since the Spanish-American war.

On the Kitsap Peninsula is the town whose site Wilkes described in 1841: "Port Orchard is one of the most beautiful of the many fine harbors on these inland waters, and is perfectly protected from the winds. The sheet of water is extensive, and is surrounded by a large growth of trees, with here and there a small prairie covered with a verdant greensward, and with its honeysuckles and roses just in bloom, resembling a well-kept lawn. The woods seem alive with squirrels, while tracks on the shore

Blockhouse at British Camp on San Juan Island dates from the "Pig War" of 1859-1872, started when an American farmer killed a British pig that was eating his potato crop; this was the only shot fired.

and through the forest showed that the larger class of animals were also in the habit of frequenting them."

Farther north on the eastern shore of the peninsula is Suquamish and the Indian burial ground which holds the grave of Chief Seattle. An inscription reads: Seattle/Chief of the Suquamish and Allied Tribes/Died June 7, 1866/The firm friend of the whites, and for him the city of Seattle was named by its founders."

A settler in the last century wrote of the reverse of the stone: "'Baptismal name, Noah Sealth/Age probably 80 years.' Indians never knew the chief by the name of Noah, the word being used probably but once, and that at the time of his baptism into the Catholic faith."

Chief Seattle was reported to be over six feet tall, a big man who towered over others both physically and spiritually. In a speech made in 1855 he said: "Every part of this soil is sacred in the estimation of my people. Every hillside, every valley, every plain and grove, has been hallowed by some sad or happy event in days long vanished. Even the rocks, which seem to be dumb and dead as they swelter in the sun along the silent shore, thrill with memories of stirring events connected with the lives of my people, and the very dust upon which you now stand responds more lovingly to their footsteps than to yours, because it is rich with the blood of our ancestors and our bare feet are conscious of the sympathetic touch. Our departed braves, fond mothers, glad, happy-hearted maidens, and even our little children who lived here and rejoiced here for a brief season, will love these somber solitudes and at eventide they greet shadowy returning spirits. And when the last Red Man shall have perished, and the memory of my tribe shall have become a myth among the White Men, these shores will swarm with the invisible dead of my tribe, and when your children's children think themselves alone in the field, the store, the shop, upon the highway, or in the silence of the pathless woods, they will not be alone. In all the earth there is no place dedicated to solitude. At night when the streets of your cities and villages are silent and you think them deserted, they will throng with the returning hosts that once filled them and

still love this beautiful land. The White Man will never be alone."

Near the eastern tip of Kitsap Peninsula is Point No Point, named by Wilkes in 1841. It was here in 1855 that the Point No Point Treaty was signed by some 50 chiefs representing the Canoe peoples of Puget Sound and Olympic Peninsula shores, among them the Snohomish, Snoqualmie, Duwamish, Chimacums and Clallam. Wilkes' geographical joke could be considered an expression not only of his disappointment with this landing place, but also of the Indians with the results of the treaty, wherein they ceded their land.

North across Admiralty Inlet is Whidbey Island, named in 1792 by Vancouver in honor of his sailing master and navigator, Joseph Whidbey. Whidbey had managed to take a boat through the turbulent waters of what Vancouver called Deception Pass because he had originally thought it led to a closed harbor. The tides rush through the narrow passage with great velocity, making the pass as treacherous for power boats today as it was for the canoes of Indians who once lived nearby. Legend tells of a young man dwelling in the waters who sought an Indian maiden. When she refused him, he stopped the salmon from coming, took away the clams and dried up the drinking water. The maiden finally married him because her people were suffering from hunger and thirst. After the marriage, he brought back the water and fish and she went to live in the tidal passage. It is said that one can still see her hair on the water, flowing back and forth with the tides.

In 1840 a Catholic mission was established on Whidbey Island by Father Francis Blanchet in response to Indians who had come to the Cowlitz mission he and Father Modeste Demers had begun in March 1839. An 1878 history recounted: "The news of the arrival of the missionary at Cowlitz caused numerous delegations of Indians to come from remote distances in order to hear and see the 'Blackgown'. Among these delegations was one led by a chief named Tsla-lacum, whose tribe inhabited Whidby Island, Puget Sound, 150 miles from the Cowlitz Mission. After a journey of two days in canoes to Fort Nesqualy, and an arduous march of three days on foot, across streams and rivers and by an exceedingly rough trail, they reached Cowlitz with bleeding feet, famished and broken down. Their object was to see the 'blackgown' and hear him speak of the great spirit.

"But the great difficulty was how to give them the idea of religion so plain and simple as to command their attention, and which they could retain in their minds and carry back with them to their tribe."

To help in his teaching, Father Blanchet created the "Catholic ladder" to tell the time of the world, the story of Christ and the events to their day. He used a piece of wood on which he made 40 marks to represent the forty centuries before Christ, 33 points for the years of Christ's life, followed by a cross, and 18 marks and 39 points for the centuries and years leading to 1839.

In 1878 history noted: "After eight days' explanation, the chief and his companions became masters of the subject; and having learned to make the sign of the cross and to sing one or two canticles in Chinook jargon, they started for home well satisfied, with a square rule thus marked, which they called Sa-ha-le stick." Later, the "ladder" was made in the form of a long chart with drawings referring to Biblical episodes, the commandments, Apostles and sacraments of the Church.

After a victorious battle with the Clallams the following year, the Indians of Whidbey Island are said to have given credit to their new-found God. In 1841, Lieutenant Wilkes told Father Blanchet that he had seen the Indians building a church beside a huge cross on Whidbey, which he called Cross Island.

The island has some 200 miles of beaches, sea-carved banks, inlets, and coves that prompt some to speak of smugglers and mysterious landings. Up from the shores, the land is rich and fertile, yielding bulbs, vegetables, berries, and grazing for dairy herds. From the cliffs you eye the San Juan Islands, the Cascades, Strait of Juan de Fuca, the Olympic Range and other islands of Puget Sound.

The San Juan Islands were first charted by Juan Francisco de Eliza in 1791 as the Isla y Archipelago de San Juan, showing those known now as San Juan, Decatur, Blakely, Orcas and Shaw as one large island. In 1792, the Galiano and Valdes expedition shortened the name to Isla de San Juan. There are well over 100 habitable islands in this once-submerged mountain chain; the oft-repeated number is 172, for those islands which occupy the waters from northern Puget Sound to Georgia Strait.

Menzies wrote on June 8, 1792: "On landing we could not help noticing the great difference between these islands and that fine country we had so lately examined, tho not removed from it above 2 or 3 leagues. Here the land rose rugged and hilly to a moderate height and was composed of massy solid rocks covered with a thin layer of blackish mould which afforded nourishment to a straddling forest of small stinted pines. The shores were almost every where steep rugged and cliffy which made landing difficult and the woods were in many places equally difficult of access from the rocky cliffs and chasms with which they abounded, but I was not at all displeased at the change and general ruggedness of the surface of the country as it produced a pleasing variety in the objects of my pursuit and added considerably to my Catalogue of Plants."

He noted two new finds: "a small well tasted wild onion which grew in little tufts in the crevices of the rocks with a species of *Arenaria* ... also ... the *Lilium Canadense* & *Lilium Camschatcense.*" You may or may not encounter the lilies of Menzies, but you will find the San Juans rich with the wildflowers, flowering shrubs and trees of the Northwest. There are the red-trunked madrone with mottled surfaces where old bark has peeled, yew, hemlock and fir; elderberry, Oregon grape and salal. Here are currant, honeysuckle and ocean spray. And where the sun peeks through shady bowers, you can look for lady's slippers, trilliums and lilies called dog tooth violets.

The waters around the islands abound with fish, from killer whales to tiny herring. On the rocks and above the waves there are gulls, cormorants and countless waterfowl, and on occasion, an eagle soaring overhead. You can follow the flights of migratory ducks and geese and look southward to vistas of Mount Rainier and the waterways leading to Puget Sound.

The *Discovery*, of the Vancouver Expedition, was anchored near the southeast point of Bainbridge Island, west of Elliott Bay, when Peter Puget accompanied by Menzies, Whidbey and a small crew began their survey of the Sound, early Sunday morning, May 20, 1792. They passed to the east of Blake Island and headed south through Colvos Passage, along the west shore of Vashon Island. Vancouver later named the island for Captain James Vashon under whom he, then a Lieutenant, and Puget, then a Midshipman, had served in Jamaica. Puget's seven-day exploration took the party through the water of the Tacoma Narrows, where, Puget later noted:

"A most rapid tide from the northward hurried us so fast past the shore that we could scarce land." They journeyed along the shores of the islands now known as Fox; Cutts, which they called Crow; McNeil, which they called Pidgeon; Ketron; Anderson; Herron, which they named Wednesday for the day they were there; Hartstene, and Squaxin. They surveyed the several inlets, went to the head of Budd Inlet where Olympia now stands and from this southerly point headed back to the *Discovery*, which they reached at 2 a.m. Sunday the 27th.

In his journal, Puget noted on various days: "a quantity of gooseberry, raspberry and currant bushes now highly in blossom which intermixed with roses, exhibited a strange varigation of flowers but by no means unpleasant to the eye ... The sky blackened ... and in a quarter of an hour every place was perfectly overcast. The squall came on with thunder, lightning and rain...though the rain had ceased yet it was succeeded by so thick a fog that the boats were scarcely perceptible from the tents."

With the decline of salmon runs and allowable fishing seasons, commercial boats are spending more time in harbor than at sea.

Vancouver retraced part of Puget's route and when he entered the harbor named Commencement Bay by Wilkes and now the port of Tacoma, he wrote in his journal: "...the perpetual clothing of snow ... seemed to form a horizontal line from north to south along this range of rugged mountains, from whose summit Mount Rainier rose conspicuously, and seemed as much elevated above them as they were above the level of the sea—the whole producing a most grand, picturesque effect."

Later, in his journal, Vancouver wrote: "Thus by our joint efforts we had completely explored every turning of this extensive inlet; and to commemorate Mr. Puget's exertions, the south extremity of it I name Puget's Sound."

In 1869, Samuel Bowles, editor of the Springfield, Massachusetts *Republican,* journeyed to study the "westward movement" and wrote: "We were a full day and night in passing down through Puget Sound to British Columbia on the steamer from Olympia, loitering along at the villages on its either shore, and studying the already considerable development of its lumber interest, as well as regaling ourselves with the beauty of its waters and its richly-stored forest shores. ... For beauty and for use this is, indeed, one of the water wonders of the world; curiosity and commerce will give it year by year increase of fame and visitors. It narrows to a river's width; it circles and swoops into the land with coquettish freedom; and then it widens into miles of breadth, carrying the largest ships anywhere on its surface, even close to the forests' edge, "free of rocks, safe from wind and wave, and home of all craft, clear, blue and fathomless."

Bowles also commented: "When the Puritans settled New England their first public duty was to build a church with thrifty thought for their souls. Out here their degenerate sons begin with organizing a restaurant and supplying Hostetter's stomachic bitters and a European or Asiatic cook. So the seat of empire in its travels westward changes its base from soul to stomach, from brains to bowels."

Restaurants continue to be organized, now with as many trained American cooks as those of other nationalities, and even the many churches raise funds with cake sales, breakfasts, dinners and salmon bakes.

The forests are now gone from the tidal shores and many of the marshlands and tide flats dredged over and claimed for building sites. Towns once solely committed to producing and shipping lumber have become cities based on diversified manufacturing. The harbors continue to greet and serve the ships of the world. Few travel the waterways today in cedar dugout canoes, but the people of these shores from Budd Inlet to Birch Bay and points in-between make the water a way of life. They commute by ferries, live on houseboats, and fill the bays, inlets and man-made moorages with their boats. It is estimated that one in four families lay claim to some type of watercraft. Even the great Boeing aircraft plant began in 1916 by making seaplanes. There are those who man the fishing fleets and those who fish from the piers and the beaches. And northeast of the San Juans, there are the Lummi Indians who have a ranch of underwater pens where they raise salmon from eggs until they reach the size for release to the waters of the sea. In 18 months, the grown salmon return to the ranch to spawn. Not all make it back home; the hazards from diseases, natural predators, and fishermen are great, but the number that do return make the venture worthwhile.

The waters are no longer as untouched as they were in Puget's day; a report based on two years study indicates that 200 toxic chemicals have been found in the Sound. The study is to continue, but its warning is already being heeded by citizens concerned about these shores and waters, and who, over the years, have managed to establish protected lands, parks, and recreation areas on the saltwater shores of the Pacific Ocean, the Strait of Juan de Fuca, Hood Canal, Puget Sound, and the San Juan Islands.

And today, the words of Menzies from almost 200 years ago still hold true: "A traveller wandering over these unfrequented plains is regaled with a salubrious and vivifying air impregnated with the balsamic fragrance of the surrounding pinery, while his mind is eagerly occupied every moment on new objects and his senses rivetted on the enchanting variety of the surrounding scenery where the softer beauties of landscape are harmoniously blended in majestic grandeur with the wild and romantic to form an interesting and picturesque prospect on every side."

Right: Pacific starfish, shown in this tidal basin near Neah Bay include an ochre starfish and a sea bat. Starfish have remarkable powers of renewal. Upon occasion, after loss of an arm the starfish will grow another one, or when cut in half, each segment may then become a new individual.

ABOUT THE PHOTOGRAPHY—
IMPRESSIONS AND DISCOVERY

Discovering and exploring the primal elements of beauty in our landscape is a total and intense experience for me...a way of life if you will. This collection of photographs is another part in an unending journey...an affair revealing my experience with light, space and time ... an unending search for eternal beauty. These photographs are personally significant because they are an important part of the universal "me" in each...an identity in a fast changing world.

The Northwest coastal province has always held a special, magical niche in my mental and photographic wanderings... a linking magnet of opposition to our Desert Southwest. The intense primal greens, overcast days, scalloped shores, scent of wet lumber or fishing fleet at anchor may have something to do with the compulsion...a compulsion to immerse myself so thoroughly in this forest/tideline province of Washington. Each of the photographs represents, visually fleeting impressions that I was experiencing in the blink of time during which the shutter was clicked. Hopefully, together they will communicate to us all a poignant and sensitive awareness to a beautiful land heritage that is ours.

Forms and textures ... sometimes elemental ... sometimes man made ... are all sensitized through our eye by the presence of "light". Light is my constant companion and tool. With an early appreciation of the Washington coastline in the 1960's, I purposely attempted, as best I could, to clear my mind of the usual influences that command creative photography work today and let my personal response bring a more intense focus on a sense of place and time. Though I work intuitively, much discipline is needed to meet the challenges of variation along the coastline. Photographic techniques were relatively simple so as not to complicate a straight forward presentation. Clear focus and sometimes brooding mood were both important tools to express varied perceptions I felt. Arrangement/Composition or positioning of objects plays a subdued role, if any at all, when presented with a potential photograph. A quick, direct response is essential or the special moment in time will slip away into eternity.

Photographs in this volume were made, with a 4 x 5 Linhof field camera, using daylight film, and 35mm Leicaflex SLR, using Kodachrome 64 film. Exposure calculations are from a Weston light meter. Lenses for 4 x 5 work are from 75mm to 500mm; for 35mm work, 19mm through 560mm. Some filtration is used sparingly to fill the gap between what I perceive and what the film actually records.

A tripod was used on all 4 x 5 work and a steady hand was relied on for the 35mm work. I like to travel light, especially on arduous treks into wilder places, so carry a limited selection of whatever equipment the situation may call for. The more I can forget the intricacies of my equipment the more concentration is available for personal expression of the subject.

Ideally the camera becomes an extension of my eye.